# VIOLIN

**HAL·LEONARD INSTRUMENTAL PLAY-ALONG**

AUDIO ACCESS INCLUDED

**PLAYBACK+**
Speed · Pitch · Balance · Loop

Disney
Beauty AND THE BEAST

To access audio visit:
**www.halleonard.com/mylibrary**

4634-8415-3695-2337

ISBN 978-1-4950-9616-7

Motion Picture Artwork, TM & Copyright
© 2017 Disney Enterprises, Inc.

**Wonderland Music Company, Inc.**
**Walt Disney Music Company**

DISTRIBUTED BY

**HAL·LEONARD®**

7777 W. BLUEMOUND RD. P.O. BOX 13819 MILWAUKEE, WI 53213

In Australia Contact:
**Hal Leonard Australia Pty. Ltd.**
4 Lentara Court
Cheltenham, Victoria, 3192 Australia
Email: ausadmin@halleonard.com.au

For all works contained herein:
Unauthorized copying, arranging, adapting, recording, Internet posting, public performance,
or other distribution of the printed or recorded music in this publication is an infringement of copyright.
Infringers are liable under the law.

Visit Hal Leonard Online at
**www.halleonard.com**

# ARIA

VIOLIN

Music by ALAN MENKEN
Lyrics by TIM RICE

© 2017 Wonderland Music Company, Inc.
All Rights Reserved. Used by Permission.

# BE OUR GUEST

VIOLIN

Music by ALAN MENKEN
Lyrics by HOWARD ASHMAN

© 1991 Wonderland Music Company, Inc. and Walt Disney Music Company
All Rights Reserved.  Used by Permission.

# BEAUTY AND THE BEAST

VIOLIN

Music by ALAN MENKEN
Lyrics by HOWARD ASHMAN

© 1991 Wonderland Music Company, Inc. and Walt Disney Music Company
All Rights Reserved. Used by Permission.

# BELLE

VIOLIN

Music by ALAN MENKEN
Lyrics by HOWARD ASHMAN

© 1991 Wonderland Music Company, Inc. and Walt Disney Music Company
All Rights Reserved. Used by Permission.

# DAYS IN THE SUN

VIOLIN

Music by ALAN MENKEN
Lyrics by TIM RICE

© 2017 Wonderland Music Company, Inc.
All Rights Reserved. Used by Permission.

# EVERMORE

VIOLIN

Music by ALAN MENKEN
Lyrics by TIM RICE

© 2017 Wonderland Music Company, Inc.
All Rights Reserved. Used by Permission.

# GASTON

VIOLIN

Music by ALAN MENKEN
Lyrics by HOWARD ASHMAN

© 1991 Wonderland Music Company, Inc. and Walt Disney Music Company
All Rights Reserved. Used by Permission.

# HOW DOES A MOMENT LAST FOREVER

VIOLIN

Music by ALAN MENKEN
Lyrics by TIM RICE

© 2017 Wonderland Music Company, Inc.
All Rights Reserved. Used by Permission.

# THE MOB SONG

VIOLIN

Music by ALAN MENKEN
Lyrics by HOWARD ASHMAN

© 1991 Wonderland Music Company, Inc. and Walt Disney Music Company
All Rights Reserved. Used by Permission.

# SOMETHING THERE

VIOLIN

Music by ALAN MENKEN
Lyrics by HOWARD ASHMAN

© 1991 Wonderland Music Company, Inc. and Walt Disney Music Company
All Rights Reserved. Used by Permission.